Content

Chapter 1: Fundamentals of Neuromarketing: Introduction to the Study of Consumer Behavior

Neuromarketing has established itself as a multidisciplinary field that merges neuroscience, marketing and psychology to understand how the human brain responds to consumption-related stimuli. In this introductory chapter, we will explore the foundations of neuromarketing and how it has become a crucial tool for understanding and shaping consumer behavior.

What is Neuromarketing?

Neuromarketing, in its essence, seeks to decipher how individuals make decisions in the field of consumption. It is based on the understanding of the brain processes that underlie purchasing choices, using techniques and tools from neuroscience to investigate the brain's response to advertising stimuli, products or purchasing experiences.

The Consumer Brain

The human brain, a marvel of evolution, is the epicenter of all the decisions and actions we carry out. Through neuroimaging and other advanced techniques, neuromarketing studies how different brain areas are activated by specific stimuli, how information is processed, and how these responses affect purchasing decisions.

Consumer Behavior: The Intersection between Science and Marketing

The study of consumer behavior is not only limited to individual preferences or tastes, but encompasses a wide range of factors. From cultural influences to psychological patterns, neuromarketing seeks to understand the complexity of purchasing decisions and how internal and external factors influence these choices.

Neuromarketing Tools and Techniques

Neuromarketing uses various tools and techniques to analyze brain responses to commercial stimuli. From functional magnetic resonance imaging (fMRI) to eye tracking and brain electrical activity (EEG) measurements, these technologies enable a deeper understanding of how information is processed in the consumer's brain.

Practical Applications of Neuromarketing

The practical application of neuromarketing extends to multiple sectors, from advertising and product design to pricing strategy and the shopping experience. Understanding how the brain responds to certain stimuli allows companies to adjust their strategies to maximize the impact on their audiences.

Ethics in Neuromarketing

With the great power to influence purchasing decisions, ethical responsibility arises in the use of neuromarketing. Reflection on the limits and transparency in the application of these techniques becomes essential to avoid manipulation and respect the autonomy of the consumer.

Conclusions

Neuromarketing emerges as a dynamic and constantly evolving field, offering a window into the complex world of the human mind in relation to consumption. Its understanding is essential for those seeking to develop effective strategies in today's market.

In summary, this introductory chapter immerses us in the essence of neuromarketing, laying the foundation to explore in detail how understanding the consumer brain is essential for success in the commercial field.

Chapter 2: Neuroscience and Marketing: Understanding the Brain-Consumption Connection

In the world of marketing, understanding how the human brain works and how it relates to purchasing decisions is essential to developing effective strategies. This chapter dives into the intersection between neuroscience and marketing, exploring how knowledge of brain activity can influence business strategies.

Neuroscience as a Tool for Marketing

Neuroscience, through advanced brain imaging techniques such as functional magnetic resonance imaging (fMRI), electroencephalogram (EEG), and eye tracking, has allowed marketers to observe and understand brain patterns in response to advertising and marketing stimuli. consumption. This provides valuable information about how information is processed in the consumer's brain.

The Decision Making Process: Neuroscientific Perspective

Decision-making regarding consumption is deeply rooted in brain activity. Neuroscience has shown that purchasing decisions are not merely rational, but are influenced by emotional, cognitive and social factors. Understanding how different brain regions are activated during this process is key to understanding and predicting consumer behavior.

Emotions and Purchase Decision: A Fundamental Link

Emotions play a crucial role in purchasing decisions. Neuroscience has revealed that strong emotions, such as happiness, surprise or fear, can significantly influence consumer preferences and their willingness to buy. Understanding how emotions affect brain activity helps design more effective advertising strategies.

Attention and Memory: Keys to Success in Marketing

Neuroscience has shown that attention and memory are vital components in the purchasing process. Understanding how to capture the consumer's attention and have the message stored in long-term memory is essential to developing successful advertising campaigns.

Neuroscience and Branding: Creating Meaningful Connections

Successful brands are able to establish emotional connections with consumers. The neuroscience of branding studies how brands activate brain areas associated with emotions and memories, thus creating lasting bonds and brand loyalty.

Ethics in the Application of Neuroscience in Marketing

The use of neuroscience in marketing raises important ethical questions. Manipulating consumer brain responses for commercial purposes sparks debates about ethics in persuasion and consumer privacy. It is essential to establish ethical limits in the application of these techniques.

Conclusions

The relationship between neuroscience and marketing offers a fascinating window into understanding how the human brain responds to commercial stimuli. The combination of these fields provides powerful tools to understand and predict consumer behavior, allowing for more effective and ethical marketing strategies.

Chapter 3: The Importance of the Emotional Brain in Purchase Decisions

In the world of neuromarketing, understanding how emotions impact purchasing decisions is essential. This chapter delves into the crucial role the emotional brain plays in consumers' decisions and how these emotions can shape and direct their purchasing choices.

Emotions and Decision Making

The human brain operates in a complex way, and many of our decisions, including purchasing decisions, are strongly influenced by emotions. Neuroscience has revealed that brain areas associated with emotions, such as the amygdala and limbic system, play a prominent role in the decision-making process.

Influence of Emotions on Brand Preferences

Emotions have a significant impact on how we perceive brands. The emotional connection with a brand can be more influential than simply evaluating its features or benefits. Brands that generate positive emotions tend to be more memorable and generate loyalty in consumers.

Effect of Emotions on Memory and Attention

Intense emotions, whether positive or negative, have the ability to capture attention and be remembered for longer. Advertising or content that evokes strong emotions tends to be more effective in terms of retention and recall.

The Power of Emotion in the Consumer Experience

The purchasing experience is deeply influenced by the emotions experienced during the process. The positive emotions associated with a pleasant shopping experience increase the likelihood that a customer will return and recommend the product or service to others.

Neuroscience of Storytelling: Creating Emotions to Drive Sales

Storytelling or the art of telling stories has become a powerful strategy in marketing. By telling stories that awaken emotions in consumers, brands can connect on an emotional level, generating empathy and increasing connection with their audience.

Emotional Strategies in Advertising and Product Design

Successful advertising campaigns often focus on evoking specific emotions in viewers. Likewise, product design and presentation can appeal to consumer emotions to generate interest and desire.

Ethical Considerations in Emotional Manipulation

Although the use of emotions in marketing can be effective, ethical debate arises about the emotional manipulation of the consumer. It is crucial to establish ethical boundaries and respect people's emotional integrity in the sales process.

Conclusions

Understanding the influence of the emotional brain on purchasing decisions is essential to developing effective marketing strategies. Emotions play a central role in consumer decision-making, and understanding them allows brands to connect more meaningfully with their audiences.

Chapter 4: Consumer Neuropsychology: Influence of Cognitive Processes on Decisions

Consumer neuropsychology focuses on understanding how cognitive and mental processes influence purchasing decisions. This field analyzes how the brain processes information, makes decisions, and evaluates options when faced with products or services on the market.

Cognitive Processes and Decision Making

The cognitive processes involved in purchasing decisions include perception, attention, memory, thinking, and decision making. Neuropsychology examines how these mental processes interact and affect the choices consumers make.

Consumer Perception and Attention

The way we perceive and pay attention to information about a product is crucial. Neuropsychology reveals how the brain filters and selects relevant information, influencing the decision to focus on certain aspects of the product over others.

Memory and Remembrance in the Purchase Process

The brain's ability to store information about products or brands is essential. Neuropsychology shows how marketing strategies can influence long-term memory and recall, ensuring that consumers remember and consider certain products when making purchasing decisions.

Thinking and Information Processing

Consumers actively process information related to a product or service before making a decision. Neuropsychology examines how this process of analysis and evaluation is carried out, including the comparison of features, benefits and prices.

Decision Making and Influencing Factors

Decision making is not a linear and rational process; It is influenced by a variety of factors. Neuropsychology studies how emotions, past experiences, cognitive biases, and social contexts impact the final purchase decision.

Neuroscience of Pricing: Pricing Strategies and Consumer Perception

The price of a product influences consumer perception. The neuropsychology of pricing analyzes how the brain responds to different pricing strategies, including the anchoring effect, value perception, and price sensitivity.

Effect of Design and Presentation on Decision Making

Product design, packaging and presentation influence how we perceive its quality and usefulness. Neuropsychology examines how the visual design and presentation of a product affects the brain response and purchase decision.

Ethical Considerations in the Influence of Cognitive Processes

Deep knowledge of the consumer's cognitive processes entails an ethical responsibility in its application. Neuropsychology highlights the importance of transparency and ethics in the use of strategies that influence purchasing decisions.

Conclusions

Consumer neuropsychology provides a comprehensive view of how the human brain processes information related to purchasing decisions. Understanding cognitive processes allows marketers to develop more effective and ethical strategies to influence consumer behavior.

Chapter 5: Sensory Neuromarketing: Impact of the Senses on Product Perception

Sensory neuromarketing focuses on how sensory stimuli impact the consumer's perception of a product or service. This field of study analyzes how the senses - sight, hearing, smell, taste and touch - influence the way we perceive, evaluate and emotionally connect with a brand or product.

The Importance of the Senses in Perception

The senses play a key role in how we experience the world around us. In the context of marketing, these senses play a crucial role in influencing consumers' perception of a product and its associated brand.

Visual Neuroscience: Impact of Sight on Product Perception

Sight is one of the most powerful senses in marketing. Visual neuromarketing studies how the colors, shapes, design and visual presentation of a product activate specific areas of the brain and shape consumer perception.

Audiomarketing: The Power of Sound in the Consumer Experience

The sense of hearing also plays a significant role in brand perception. Music, sounds, jingles and auditory effects used in advertising campaigns can generate emotions and memories, impacting the purchase decision.

Olfactomarketing: Aroma as a Persuasive Tool

The sense of smell has the ability to evoke emotions and memories in powerful ways. The strategic use of aromas in stores, commercial spaces or products can influence consumer perception and experience.

Gustomarketing: Flavor as an Influencing Factor

The sense of taste can also influence the perception of the product. Tasting strategies, free samples or specific flavors can impact quality perception and generate preference for certain products.

Haptomarketing: Touch in the Consumer Experience

The sense of touch can be a differentiating factor in the perception of the product. Design, texture and material quality can influence the consumer's tactile experience and their evaluation of the product.

Synesthesia in Neuromarketing: Combining Senses to Impact

Synesthesia, which is the combination of different senses, can enhance the consumer experience. Strategies that combine multiple sensory stimuli can generate a more immersive and memorable experience.

Practical Applications in Sensory Neuromarketing

The practical applications of sensory neuromarketing extend to multiple industries. From the food industry to fashion and technology, strategic use of the senses can differentiate a product and improve the connection with the consumer.

Ethics in Sensory Neuromarketing

Using the senses for commercial purposes raises ethical questions about manipulation and transparency. It is essential to establish ethical boundaries when influencing consumer perception through the senses.

Conclusions

Sensory neuromarketing offers deep insight into how the senses impact product and brand perception. Understanding how sensory stimuli affect the consumer experience allows us to develop more effective marketing strategies focused on emotional connection.

Chapter 6: Visual Marketing: The Power of Images and Neuroaesthetics

Visual marketing is a powerful tool in the world of neuromarketing. This chapter dives into the neuroscience behind visual perception, the influence of images on purchasing decisions, and the importance of neuroaesthetics in designing effective consumer experiences.

The Importance of Images in Marketing

Images have a profound impact on consumer perception and memory. Neuroscience reveals that the human brain processes visual information more quickly and effectively than other types of content, making images a valuable tool in marketing.

Neuroscience of Visual Perception

Visual perception is based on how the brain interprets the information it receives through the eyes. Visual neuroscience studies how colors, shapes, patterns and visual details are processed and recognized, and how this affects consumer perception.

Impact of Images on Emotions and Memory

Images have the power to evoke emotions and create lasting memories. Neuroscience shows that emotional images activate brain areas related to emotions, making these images more memorable and having a more significant impact on decision making.

Neuroaesthetics: The Art of Visual Beauty and Its Influence

Neuroaesthetics focuses on how the brain perceives and experiences visual beauty. The aesthetic design of images and visual elements in marketing can generate positive emotional responses in the consumer's brain, influencing their perception of the brand or product.

Colors and Their Impact on Consumer Behavior

Colors have a significant psychological effect on consumer perception and emotional response. Color neuroscience looks at how different colors can influence emotions, attention, and purchasing decisions.

Visual Design and User Experience (UX)

Visual design plays a crucial role in user experience in digital and physical environments. The neuroscience of experience design looks at how visual design can impact ease of use, user satisfaction, and emotional connection to a product or service.

Impact of Images in Advertising and Branding

Images used in advertising and branding have a lasting impact on the consumer's mind. The neuroscience of visual branding explores how images can communicate brand identity, build trust, and foster customer loyalty.

Ethics in the Use of Images and Neuroaesthetics

The use of neuroaesthetic imaging and techniques raises ethical questions about authenticity and manipulation. It is crucial to balance the effectiveness of visual design with the ethical responsibility of not deceiving or manipulating the consumer.

Conclusions

Visual marketing and neuroaesthetics are fundamental components in creating effective consumer experiences. Understanding how images impact consumer perception allows marketers to develop more impactful and ethical visual strategies.

Chapter 7: Neurology of Color: Chromatic Strategies in Marketing

The strategic use of color is essential in the world of neuromarketing. This chapter explores the neurology behind how colors affect consumers' emotions, perceptions, and decisions in the field of marketing.

The Power of Color in Marketing

Colors play a vital role in consumers' perception and emotional response towards products and brands. Color neurology studies how different shades and combinations affect brain response and decision making.

Emotions and Responses Associated with Colors

Each color has the ability to evoke specific emotions in consumers. Neurology reveals how red can generate excitement, blue conveys confidence, green is associated with freshness and nature, among other emotional effects.

Influence of Colors on Brand Perception

Colors also play an important role in the perception of a brand. The choice of colors in branding can influence how a brand's identity, values and personality are perceived, generating an emotional connection with consumers.

Strategies for Using Colors in Marketing

Color strategies in marketing are applied in the design of logos, packaging, websites, advertising and more. The neurology of color explores how the right choice of colors can influence consumer attention, interest, and action.

Color Psychology and Consumer Behavior

Color psychology shows how consumers unconsciously react to color stimuli. Colors can influence purchasing decisions, time spent on a website, perception of quality, and perceived value of a product.

Colors in Different Industries and Cultures

Color perception can vary between different industries and cultures. Color neurology examines how colors are interpreted in different cultural contexts and how they can have different meanings and associations in various regions of the world.

Color Neuroscience in Advertising and Graphic Design

Color neuroscience in advertising and graphic design studies how colors can influence consumer attention, memory, and persuasion. Strategies such as contrast, chromatic harmony and focusing are used to maximize visual impact.

Ethics in the Use of Chromatic Strategies

Despite the powerful influence of color, it is essential to apply ethical strategies in marketing. The use of colors should not induce manipulation or confusion of the consumer, but rather serve as a tool to communicate effectively.

Conclusions

The neurology of color demonstrates how colors have a profound impact on consumer perceptions and decisions in marketing. Understanding the influence of colors allows marketers to develop more effective and meaningful visual strategies.

Chapter 8: Auditory Neuromarketing: Sound as a Persuasive Tool

Auditory neuromarketing focuses on how sound and auditory stimuli impact consumer emotions, purchasing decisions, and perception. This chapter explores how sound becomes a powerful persuasive tool in marketing strategies.

The Power of Sound in Marketing

Sound is a powerful tool to influence consumers' emotions and decisions. Auditory neuroscience shows how sound stimuli affect the brain and can generate deep emotional responses.

Neuroscience of Sound and Emotions

Neuroscience has shown that sounds can evoke specific emotions in consumers. From music to sound effects, different tones and frequencies can trigger emotional responses that influence consumer perception.

Music as an Emotional Tool in Marketing

Music has the power to influence the emotions and mood of consumers. Auditory neuroscience explores how the choice of music in advertisements, stores or websites can impact the consumer's experience and connection to the brand.

Auditory Effects on Memory and Attention

Sounds can improve information retention and consumer attention. The neuroscience of sound shows how auditory effects can help highlight key messages and make consumers better remember a product or brand.

Sound Strategies in Advertising

In advertising, sound effects, jingles, and auditory narratives are used strategically to create an emotional connection with the audience. These strategies seek to awaken emotions and generate a lasting impact.

Sound Narratives and Storytelling

Auditory storytelling is a powerful technique in neuromarketing. Creating sound narratives and immersive audio experiences can engage consumers in a deeper way, generating stronger emotional connections.

Sound Neuromarketing in Different Industrial Sectors

Auditory neuromarketing is applied in a wide range of industries, from advertising to retail, entertainment and telephony. The sounds are strategically designed to improve the consumer experience and strengthen the relationship with the brand.

Ethics in the Use of Auditory Neuromarketing

Despite its persuasive power, it is essential to apply auditory neuromarketing ethically. Sounds should not be misleading or manipulative, but rather enhance the consumer experience in a transparent and authentic way.

Conclusions

Auditory neuromarketing demonstrates how sound can be a persuasive tool in marketing. Understanding how auditory stimuli affect consumer emotions and behavior allows for the development of more effective and emotionally impactful marketing strategies.

Chapter 9: The Psychology of Price: How the Brain Responds to Pricing Strategies

Price psychology is a crucial field in neuromarketing that explores how consumers' brains respond to different pricing strategies. This chapter explores in detail how pricing strategies influence consumers' perceptions and purchasing decisions.

Value Perception and Pricing Strategies

The way in which the price of a product is presented influences the perception of its value. Strategies such as price anchoring, numbering, comparison, and discounting strategies can change the way consumers value a product.

Neuroscience of Price: How the Brain Processes Price Information

Neuroscience reveals that consumers' brains respond differently to various types of prices. Studies show how certain prices activate brain areas associated with reward, pleasure or the perception of a bargain.

Effect of Context on Price Perception

The context in which the price is presented can significantly influence consumer perception. Price neuroscience studies how factors such as place, time, and presentation affect how a price is perceived.

Price Sensitivity and Pricing Strategies

Price sensitivity varies among consumers. The neuroscience of pricing looks at how dynamic pricing, psychological pricing (99, 199), or premium pricing strategies can impact different consumer segments.

Discount and Promotion Strategies

Discounts and promotions have a significant effect on consumer behavior. Neuroscience reveals how percentage discounts, coupons, or "buy one, get one free" deals influence purchasing decision making.

Prices and Quality Perception

Price can serve as an indicator of quality for consumers. The neuroscience of price explores how consumers associate a higher price with higher quality and how this perception can influence their purchasing decisions.

Impact of Decimals and Fractions on Price Perception

The choice between round prices and prices that end in decimals can have an impact on consumer perception. The neuroscience of price shows how exact prices can be perceived as cheaper and more attractive.

Ethics in Pricing

The use of pricing strategies raises ethical questions. It is crucial to apply pricing strategies in a transparent and ethical manner, avoiding deceptive or manipulative practices that could negatively affect consumer trust.

Conclusions

Price psychology is fundamental in neuromarketing, understanding how pricing strategies affect consumer perceptions and decisions. Understanding the brain's response to prices allows marketers to develop more effective and ethical pricing strategies.

Chapter 10: Neuromarketing in Packaging and Label Design

Neuromarketing in packaging and label design is a field that studies how the visual design of packaging and labels influences consumer purchasing decisions. This chapter will explore in detail how the design of these elements can impact consumer perception and preference.

The Role of Packaging and Label Design in Neuromarketing

Packaging and labels are key elements in the perception of a product. Neuroscience applied to design shows how these elements can influence consumer emotions, attention, and decision-making.

Visual Neuroscience Applied to Packaging Design

Visual neuroscience examines how graphic design, typography, colors, and the arrangement of information on a package or label affect consumer perception and attraction to the product.

Impact of Shape and Texture on Packaging Perception

The shape and texture of a container have a significant impact on tactile and visual perception. The neuroscience of packaging design examines how these characteristics can influence quality perception and consumer preference.

Color Psychology in Labels and Packaging

The colors used on labels and packaging can influence consumer emotions and associations. Color psychology applied to design helps convey messages and create emotional connections with consumers.

Label Design and Cognitive Scannability

The ease of scanning and understanding the information on a label is crucial. The neuroscience of label design examines how the arrangement of information can facilitate consumer decision-making at the point of sale.

Impact of Visual Storytelling on Packaging and Labels

Visual storytelling on packaging and labels tells a story about the product. Neuroscience applied to visual storytelling shows how this approach can generate emotional connections and highlight the values of the product.

Packaging Design for Different Consumer Segments

Packaging design can be adapted to different consumer segments. Design neuroscience considers how the preferences and sensitivities of each demographic group can influence the design to better appeal to them.

Technology and Design of Interactive Packaging

The incorporation of technology in the design of packaging and labels offers new opportunities. The neuroscience of interactive design examines how augmented reality or QR codes can improve the consumer experience.

Ethics in Packaging and Label Design

It is essential to apply ethical principles in the design of packaging and labels. Neuromarketing must be used in a transparent and respectful manner, avoiding deceptive or manipulative practices that could harm consumer trust.

Conclusions

Neuromarketing applied to packaging and label design demonstrates how visual elements can influence consumer perception and preference. Understanding how design impacts the consumer's brain allows us to develop more effective and ethical strategies.

Chapter 11: Neuroscience of Storytelling: The Art of Connecting with the Consumer's Brain through Narratives

Storytelling, or the art of telling stories, is a powerful tool in neuromarketing. This chapter explores in detail how narratives impact the consumer's brain, influencing their emotions, perceptions, and purchasing decisions.

The Power of Stories in Neuromarketing

Stories have the ability to capture the consumer's attention and generate an emotional connection. The neuroscience of storytelling reveals how narratives activate brain areas associated with empathy, memory and decision making.

Brain Neuroscience and Stories

The human brain is wired to respond to stories. Neuroscience shows that narratives trigger the release of neurotransmitters such as dopamine, which sparks interest and creates an emotional connection to the content.

Emotions and Empathy in Storytelling

Stories that evoke emotions are more memorable. Neuroscience shows how emotional narratives can generate empathy in consumers, making them feel a greater connection to the characters and story.

Impact of Narratives on Memory

Stories told well are easier to remember. The neuroscience of storytelling highlights how compellingly structured narratives can increase information retention and improve brand or product recall.

Construction of Narratives in Marketing

Effective marketing is based on building persuasive stories. The neuroscience of storytelling in marketing explores how to create authentic and relevant narratives that connect with audiences and generate an emotional response.

Key Elements of Effective Storytelling

Structure, characters, conflicts and resolutions are essential elements in effective storytelling. The neuroscience of storytelling analyzes how these elements can influence the response of the consumer's brain.

Adaptation of Storytelling to Different Media

Storytelling can be adapted to various formats, from television advertisements to content on social networks or websites. The neuroscience of storytelling considers how to adjust stories for each specific medium and audience.

Neuroscience of Engagement through Interactive Stories

Interactive stories involve the consumer in the narrative process. The neuroscience of interactive storytelling shows how these participatory experiences increase engagement and emotional connection with the brand.

Ethics in the Use of Storytelling in Marketing

The use of storytelling in marketing must be ethical and authentic. It is essential to maintain truthfulness and transparency in narratives, avoiding manipulations or false representations that could affect consumer confidence.

Conclusions

Effective storytelling in neuromarketing has a significant impact on consumer perception and response. Understanding how stories influence the consumer's brain allows us to develop more effective and emotionally persuasive strategies.

Chapter 12: Digital Marketing: Impact of Online Strategies on the Consumer's Mind

Digital marketing has transformed the way brands connect with consumers. In this chapter, we will explore how online strategies affect the consumer's mind from the perspective of neuromarketing and behavioral psychology.

Evolution of Marketing in the Digital Environment

The rise of digital marketing has changed the way brands interact with consumers. Adaptation to new online platforms and channels has allowed more direct and immediate communication.

Neuroscience of User Experience (UX) Online

The user experience in digital environments is essential. The neuroscience of UX analyzes how web design, navigation, and interactivity affect consumer perception and engagement with the brand.

Personalization and Segmentation in Online Strategies

Content personalization and audience segmentation are key strategies in digital marketing. Neuroscience shows how tailoring messages to individual interests improves consumer response.

Impact of Social Networks on Consumer Behavior

Social networks are powerful platforms in digital marketing. The neuroscience of social media explores how content, interaction, and social media influence impact purchasing decisions and brand perception.

Neuromarketing in Online Advertising

Online advertising adapts to consumer behaviors and preferences. The neuroscience of digital advertising shows how interactive ads, videos and banners impact consumer attention and memory.

Neuropsychology of E-mail Marketing and Automation

Email marketing and campaign automation have an impact on the consumer's mind. The neuropsychology of email marketing analyzes how personalized emails influence purchasing decisions.

Neurosales and Neuromarketing in eCommerce

ECommerce benefits from neuromarketing strategies. The neuroscience of online sales explores how product presentation, colors, and the simplicity of the purchasing process affect consumer decisions.

Cognition and Decision Making in Content Marketing

Content marketing is based on understanding consumer cognition. The neuroscience of content marketing shows how storytelling, infographics and videos impact understanding and decision making.

Integration of Emerging Technologies in Digital Marketing

Emerging technologies such as augmented reality or artificial intelligence are transforming digital marketing. The neuroscience of these technologies shows how they influence the consumer experience.

Ethics in Digital Marketing

The ethical use of digital strategies is essential. It is crucial to apply neuromarketing and digital strategies in a transparent manner, respecting privacy and avoiding manipulative or invasive practices.

Conclusions

Digital marketing has a profound impact on the consumer's mind. Understanding how online strategies influence consumer emotions, perceptions and decisions allows us to develop more effective and ethical strategies in the digital environment.

Chapter 13: Social Neuromarketing: Influence of Social Networks on Purchasing Behavior

Social media has revolutionized the way people connect, communicate and interact with the world. From a neuromarketing point of view, the impact of these platforms on purchasing behavior is significant and deserves detailed exploration.

Neuroscience of Interaction in Social Networks

Social networks activate brain areas associated with gratification and social interaction. These platforms trigger the release of dopamine, generating a feeling of pleasure and connection when interacting with content or receiving likes and comments.

Influence of Social Networks on Purchase Decisions

Social media plays a crucial role in the purchasing decision-making process. The opinions of friends, influencers and reviews impact the perception of a product or service, influencing an individual's purchase intention.

Neuroscience of Viral and Engageable Content

Content on social networks has the ability to go viral. Neuroscience shows how content that arouses intense emotions, is shareable and provokes active interaction can spread quickly, affecting the perception of a brand or product.

Effect of Advertising on Social Networks on the Consumer's Mind

Advertising on social platforms adapts to the user's preferences and behaviors. The neuroscience of network advertising shows how personalized and relevant ads impact memory and decision making.

Influencers and their Neuroemotional Impact on the Consumer

Influencers have significant power in influencing purchasing behavior. Neuroscience shows how the emotional connection with an influencer can affect the perception of a product and the consumer's purchase intention.

Feedback and Social Proof in Social Networks

Feedback and social validation are important in purchasing decisions. Neuroscience shows how likes, comments and reviews act as "social proof", affecting the perception of trust in a product or service.

Use of Neurodata for Optimization in Social Networks

The collection of data on social networks allows the optimization of strategies. The neuroscience of social data looks at how to use this information to personalize content, segment audiences, and improve the impact of campaigns.

Ethics in Social Neuromarketing

The ethical use of social media strategies is crucial. It is necessary to respect the user's privacy, avoid excessive manipulation and guarantee transparency in communication to build a relationship of trust with the consumer.

Conclusions

Social media has a profound impact on purchasing behavior. Understanding how these platforms influence consumer emotions, perceptions and decisions allows us to develop more effective and ethical marketing strategies in social environments.

Chapter 14: Neuromarketing in Advertising: Effective Techniques to Stimulate Brain Response

Advertising is a key field in neuromarketing, as it seeks to understand how to stimulate brain responses that impact consumers' emotions, perceptions and decisions. This chapter explores the effective techniques used in advertising from a neuromarketing perspective.

Fundamentals of Neuromarketing in Advertising

Neuromarketing in advertising is based on understanding how the brain responds to specific stimuli. Research in cognitive and behavioral neuroscience allows us to develop more effective advertising strategies.

Neuroscience of Visual Appeal in Advertising

Visual design in advertising triggers brain responses. Neuroscience reveals how colors, shapes, images and graphic design impact the attraction and retention of consumer attention.

Impact of Emotions in Neuromarketing Advertising

Emotions play a crucial role in effective advertising. Neuroscience shows how the generation of positive emotions or the emotional connection with advertising content influences the consumer's brain response.

Neuromarketing in the Creation of Persuasive Messages

Advertising messages can be optimized to maximize their impact. The neuroscience of language reveals how the structure, words and tone in advertising messages affect the consumer's brain response.

Use of Neuroimaging in the Study of Advertising

Neuroimaging techniques, such as functional magnetic resonance imaging (fMRI), allow us to study brain activity when faced with advertisements. These tools help to better understand brain responses to advertising.

Effectiveness of Audiovisual Advertising in Neuromarketing

Audiovisual advertising has a great impact. Neuroscience shows how the combination of images and sound in television advertisements or online videos influences memory and perception of the message.

Neuroscience of Interactive Advertising

Interactive advertising stimulates consumer participation. Neuroscience shows how interactions in digital ads or interactive advertising experiences impact the consumer's brain response.

Influence of Neuromarketing on Media Strategy

Neuroscience guides the choice of more effective advertising media. Analyzes how consumer behavior on different channels and platforms impacts the brain response to advertising.

Ethical Neuromarketing in Advertising

It is essential to use neuromarketing ethically in advertising. Respecting consumer privacy, avoiding excessive manipulation and ensuring transparency in advertising strategies is essential.

Conclusions

Neuromarketing applied to advertising seeks to understand and stimulate brain responses that influence consumers' emotions, perceptions and decisions. Its effective and ethical application can lead to more impactful and successful advertising strategies.

Chapter 15: Neuromarketing and Neuroleadership: Applications in Business Management

Neuromarketing and neuroleadership are interconnected areas that find valuable applications in business management. This chapter explores how neuromarketing strategies and neuroleadership principles can influence business decision-making and team management.

Fundamentals of Neuromarketing and Neuroleadership

Neuromarketing focuses on understanding how the consumer's brain responds to marketing stimuli, while neuroleadership focuses on applying insights from the brain to team management and leadership. Both have neuroscientific bases that seek to optimize results.

Applications of Neuromarketing in Business Management

Neuromarketing can be applied in business management to better understand customers, develop more effective sales strategies, and design products that align with market preferences. Use consumer behavior data to make strategic decisions.

Neuroleadership and its Impact on Team Management

Neuroleadership focuses on understanding how the human brain responds to leadership and how this knowledge can be applied to motivate, inspire, and lead work teams more effectively. Consider the importance of empathy, motivation and communication in leadership.

Decision Making based on Neuromarketing Principles

Business decisions can be influenced by neuromarketing principles. Understanding how consumer emotions, perception and decision-making can affect business strategies allows for more informed and accurate decisions.

Leadership and Effective Communication based on Neuroleadership

Neuroleadership considers how communication, setting clear goals, and building effective relationships can optimize team performance. He focuses on leading from an empathetic and motivating position.

Neuroscience applied to Organizational Culture

Neuroscience can also inform how to design an effective organizational culture. Understand how the brain responds to work environments and how to promote collaboration, innovation and emotional well-being at work.

Motivation and Commitment Strategies based on Neurological Principles

Neuroleadership considers strategies to motivate and engage employees using neurological principles. Explore how rewards, recognition and autonomy can increase motivation and engagement in the work environment.

Ethical Applications of Neuromarketing and Neuroleadership

It is essential to apply both neuromarketing and neuroleadership ethically in the business environment. The privacy, integrity and rights of employees and customers must be respected in all strategies implemented.

Conclusions

The combination of neuromarketing and neuroleadership offers valuable tools for business management. Understanding how the human brain responds to marketing and leadership stimuli allows companies to optimize their strategies and foster more effective and motivating work environments.

Chapter 16: Ethics in Neuromarketing: Limits and Responsibilities in Brain Influence

Neuromarketing, by harnessing knowledge about the functioning of the human brain in the context of marketing and advertising, raises important ethical questions about the limit of influence and responsibility in consumer behavior.

Ethical Foundations of Neuromarketing

Ethical neuromarketing is based on respect for privacy, transparency and honesty in influence strategies. It seeks to balance business objectives with consumer well-being and rights.

Privacy and Consumer Consent

Respect for consumer privacy is essential in neuromarketing. Informed consent regarding the use of neurological data to influence purchasing decisions is essential to maintain ethics in these practices.

Manipulation versus Persuasive Information

The line between ethical persuasion and manipulation in neuromarketing is delicate. Practices that seek to improperly manipulate consumer decisions must be avoided, ensuring that the information provided is clear and truthful.

Ethics in Advertising and Subliminal Messages

The use of subliminal techniques raises ethical dilemmas. It is crucial to ensure that advertising messages are ethical and do not seek to subconsciously or manipulatively influence consumer decisions without informed consent.

Respect for Diversity and Cultural Sensitivity

Ethical neuromarketing considers cultural diversity and the ethical values of different social groups. Avoid strategies that may be offensive or discriminatory, respecting the cultural sensitivity of each audience.

Corporate Social Responsibility in Neuromarketing

Companies have the responsibility to contribute positively to society. Ethical neuromarketing promotes strategies that not only seek to maximize economic benefits, but also take into account social and environmental impact.

Transparency in the Communication of Neuromarketing Practices

Transparency is key in ethical neuromarketing. Companies must clearly and accessible communicate the neurological strategies used in their advertising campaigns, providing adequate information to consumers.

Regulation and Ethical Standards in Neuromarketing

The implementation of ethical regulations and standards is important to maintain ethical practices in neuromarketing. Establishing ethical standards and oversight helps protect consumer rights and privacy.

Education and Awareness on Ethical Neuromarketing

Promoting education and awareness about ethical neuromarketing is essential. Both consumers and professionals in the field of marketing must understand the ethical limits and implications of neurological strategies on consumer behavior.

Conclusions

Ethical neuromarketing seeks to balance brain influence with responsibility and respect for consumers. Promotes transparent, respectful and socially responsible practices to ensure that brain influence is used ethically and non-invasively.

Chapter 17: Neurosales: Strategies to Optimize the Sales Process

Neurosales focuses on understanding consumer behavior from a neuroscientific perspective to improve sales strategies and enhance effectiveness in the marketing process. These strategies use insights into how the brain makes decisions to optimize sales.

Neuroscience behind Purchase Decisions

Neuroscience reveals that purchasing decisions are not exclusively rational, but are influenced by emotions and subconscious processes. Understanding these aspects allows us to develop more effective sales strategies.

Emotions and Sales: Deep Connection

Emotions play a crucial role in sales. Neuroscience shows how generating positive emotions in customers can increase the probability of closing sales, due to the emotional connection with the product or service.

Neuroscience of the Customer Decision Making Process

The purchasing decision-making process is influenced by areas of the brain related to emotion and memory. Understanding these processes allows you to adapt sales strategies to influence customer decisions.

Persuasion Techniques based on Neuroscience

Persuasion techniques are based on neuroscientific principles. Factors such as scarcity, authority, reciprocity and consistency are elements that, when applied correctly, can influence the customer's purchasing decision.

Neuroscience in Sales Communication

Neuroscience helps us understand how to effectively communicate the benefits of a product or service. Establishing a compelling narrative, using persuasive language, and showing empathy can influence a customer's purchasing decision.

Optimization of the Purchasing Environment based on Neuroscience

The purchasing environment can influence customers' decisions. The layout of the space, visual presentation and music can be adjusted to create a more conducive environment for selling.

Neurosales in Customer Experience

Neurosales strategies seek to improve the customer experience. Understanding how the customer perceives and experiences the purchasing process allows us to optimize each stage to increase satisfaction and loyalty.

Integration of Technology in Neurosales Strategies

Technology can enhance neurosales strategies. Data analytics, artificial intelligence and augmented reality can be used to better understand customer behavior and adapt sales strategies.

Ethics in Neurosales

It is crucial to apply neurosales ethically. Respecting client privacy, avoiding manipulation and providing truthful information are fundamental principles to maintain ethics in these strategies.

Conclusions

Neurosales seeks to understand customer behavior from a neurological perspective to optimize sales strategies. By understanding how the human brain influences purchasing decisions, more effective and ethical strategies can be developed in the marketing process.

Chapter 18: Neuromarketing in Retail: Improving the Shopping Experience in Physical Stores

Neuromarketing applied to the retail environment focuses on understanding how consumers' brains respond to specific stimuli within physical stores. This chapter explores strategies and techniques based on neuroscience to improve the shopping experience in these spaces.

Understanding Consumer Behavior in Retail

Consumer behavior in commercial environments is influenced by sensory, emotional and cognitive factors. Neuromarketing seeks to understand how these factors impact purchasing decisions in physical stores.

Store Design based on Neuroscience

The design of the retail environment can be optimized using principles of neuroscience. Factors such as space layout, lighting, colors, music and signage can influence the customer experience and purchasing decisions.

Sensory Neuromarketing in Retail

Sensory neuromarketing harnesses the senses to create memorable in-store experiences. Smells, textures, sounds and visual stimuli are used strategically to stimulate emotions and create connections with products.

Product Optimization and Presentation at the Point of Sale

The presentation of products at the point of sale can be improved using knowledge from neuroscience. Strategies such as positioning, product organization and packaging can influence consumer perception and preference.

Emotional Stimulus and Brand Experience

Emotions play a key role in the shopping experience. Neuromarketing seeks to create positive emotional experiences that strengthen the emotional connection between the consumer and the brand, encouraging loyalty.

Use of Technology in the Retail Environment

Technology can be an ally in retail neuromarketing. From the use of sensors to analyze customer behavior to the implementation of augmented reality to improve interaction and purchasing experience.

Personalization of the Shopping Experience

Neuromarketing seeks to personalize the shopping experience in physical stores. Strategies such as customer segmentation, using data, and tailoring offers can meet individual needs and increase customer satisfaction.

Measurement and Data Analysis in Neuroscientific Retail

Data collection and analysis play a crucial role. Tools such as eye tracking, facial expression monitoring, and surveys can provide valuable information to understand consumer behavior in retail.

Ethics in the Implementation of Neuromarketing in Retail

It is essential to apply neuromarketing in retail in an ethical manner. Respecting consumer privacy, being transparent in the practices implemented and avoiding improper manipulation are key principles to maintain ethics in these strategies.

Conclusions

Neuromarketing in retail seeks to improve the shopping experience in physical stores by understanding and applying knowledge of neuroscience in the design, product presentation, emotional stimulation and use of technology. Applied ethically, it can enhance customer satisfaction and sales effectiveness.

Chapter 19: Neurofeedback and Marketing: Using Brain Feedback in Business Strategies

Neurofeedback, a technique that allows brain activity to be observed in real time, has become a valuable tool for understanding consumers' brain responses to commercial stimuli. This chapter explores how this technique is applied in marketing and sales strategies.

Fundamentals of Neurofeedback and its Relationship with Marketing

Neurofeedback is a method that uses neuroimaging devices to monitor brain activity. In the context of marketing, it is used to capture consumers' brain reactions to product stimuli or advertising campaigns.

Technology and Methods in Neurofeedback Applied to Marketing

The technology used in neurofeedback has evolved, allowing for more precise and accessible monitoring of brain activity. Techniques such as functional magnetic resonance imaging (fMRI), electroencephalography (EEG) and near-infrared spectroscopy (NIRS) are applied to analyze brain responses in the commercial environment.

Consumer Behavior through Neurofeedback

Neurofeedback allows us to understand in real time how the brain responds to specific stimuli. Analyzes attention, emotions, associative memories and other cognitive processes that impact consumer purchasing decisions.

Applications of Neurofeedback in Product Development

Neurofeedback is used in product development to assess consumer receptivity. It allows you to identify attractive features and areas of improvement in products and services through direct observation of brain responses.

Neurofeedback in the Evaluation of Advertising Campaigns

Neurofeedback is useful for evaluating the effectiveness of advertising campaigns. It allows you to identify which elements of a campaign activate positive responses in the consumer's brain, facilitating adjustments to increase its impact.

Personalization of Marketing Strategies with Neurofeedback

Neurofeedback makes it possible to personalize marketing strategies. By understanding individual brain preferences, companies can tailor their messages and products to achieve greater resonance with their customers.

Success in Sales and Neurofeedback

Neurofeedback contributes to sales success by optimizing marketing strategies. Companies can use the information obtained to make more informed and effective decisions, maximizing the impact of their business initiatives.

Ethical Challenges in the Use of Neurofeedback in Marketing

The use of neurofeedback raises ethical challenges, including privacy and consumer consent. It is essential to ensure that the rights and integrity of the individual are respected in the collection and use of brain data.

Future of Neurofeedback in Marketing

Neurofeedback promises an exciting future in the world of marketing. Its continued application can lead to more precise and personalized marketing, improving the consumer experience and the effectiveness of commercial strategies.

Conclusions

The use of neurofeedback in business strategies offers a window into consumer brain behavior, allowing companies to understand and adjust their marketing and sales strategies more accurately and effectively, as long as it is applied ethically and with due respect to the privacy of the individual.

Chapter 20: Neuroplasticity and Change in Consumption Habits

Neuroplasticity, the brain's ability to change and adapt, offers a promising perspective for understanding and changing consumer habits. This chapter explores how the concept of neuroplasticity can be applied to modify consumption patterns.

Neuroplasticity and Brain Adaptation

Neuroplasticity refers to the brain's ability to reorganize and change in response to experience and learning. This ability allows the brain to adapt to new circumstances and learn new skills.

Consumption Habits and Neural Connections

Consumption habits are rooted in the neural connections of the brain. They are formed through repetition and the association between stimuli and responses, generating neural connections that reinforce these behaviors.

Understanding Habit Formation from a Neurological Perspective

Habit formation is related to the consolidation of specific neural circuits. These circuits become stronger with repetition, making behaviors automatic and difficult to change.

Neuroplasticity and Possibility of Changing Habits

Despite the ingrained nature of habits, neuroplasticity suggests that the brain is malleable and adaptable. New neural connections can be created and existing habits modified through specific strategies.

Techniques to Modify Habits from the Perspective of Neuroplasticity

Habit modification can be facilitated using approaches based on neuroplasticity. Strategies such as mindful repetition, clear goal setting, behavior replacement, and visualization can help change habits.

Neuroscience Applied to Changing Consumption Habits

The application of neuroscience in changing consumer habits involves understanding how certain stimuli and rewards activate specific areas of the brain. Identifying and manipulating these neural circuits can facilitate the modification of habits.

Personalization of Habit Change Strategies

Personalization is key to effective habit change. Understanding neuroplasticity makes it possible to adapt change strategies to the individual characteristics of each person, maximizing effectiveness.

Time and Persistence in Changing Habits according to Neuroplasticity

Changing habits takes time and persistence. Neuroplasticity suggests that repetition and consistency are essential for establishing new neural connections and consolidating new behavioral patterns.

Practical Applications of Knowledge of Neuroplasticity in Consumption

Knowledge about neuroplasticity can be applied in various areas of consumption, such as the adoption of healthy habits, the reduction of compulsive consumption or the promotion of more conscious purchasing decisions.

Ethics in the Application of Neuroplasticity in Consumption

It is essential to apply ethical principles when using knowledge about neuroplasticity in consumption. Respecting privacy, informed consent and avoiding manipulation are essential in the implementation of strategies based on neuroplasticity.

Conclusions

Understanding neuroplasticity offers a powerful approach to understanding and changing consumer habits. Using strategies based on brain plasticity, it is possible to modify deep-seated patterns, promoting more conscious and healthy consumption, as long as it is applied in an ethical and respectful manner.

Chapter 21: Neuromarketing: Success and Failure - Lessons from Memorable Campaigns and Common Mistakes

Neuromarketing offers a unique window to analyze successful advertising campaigns and common mistakes that have marked the history of marketing. This chapter explores notable examples of both extremes and the valuable lessons that can be drawn from them.

Success in Neuromarketing Campaigns: Lessons Learned

1. **Coca-Cola and Emotion:**Coca-Cola's longevity is attributed to its ability to evoke positive emotions and associate with shared experiences.

2. **Apple and the Power of Narrative:**The story behind Apple, focused on creativity and innovation, has created a community of loyal followers.

3. **Nike and Inspiration:**Campaigns like "Just Do It" focus on inspiring through powerful narratives that go beyond the product.

4. **Dove and Authenticity:**Focus on campaigns that promote self-acceptance and diversity, connecting emotionally with your audience.

5. **Amazon and Customer Experience:**Their relentless focus on customer experience and convenience has been key to their success.

Common Mistakes in Neuromarketing Campaigns: Lessons to Consider

1. **Pepsi and the Controversy:**The Pepsi campaign with Kendall Jenner failed by trying to capitalize on sensitive social issues without authenticity.

2. **McDonald's and Misperception:**Failed attempts to change your image without fully understanding the client's expectations.

3. **Colgate and the Misinterpretation:**A campaign involving ice cream with toothpaste, which was perceived confusingly by the public.

4. **Red Bull and Exclusivity:**Exploit aggressive marketing strategies, sometimes alienating certain segments of the audience.

5. **New Coke and Lack of Emotional Connection:**A classic example of changing a beloved product without considering the consumer's emotional connection.

Key Lessons from Successful and Failed Campaigns

1. **Know your Audience:**Successful campaigns understand their target audience on an emotional and cognitive level.

2. **Authenticity and Coherence:**Authenticity in the message and consistency with the brand identity are essential.

3. **Emotions and Connection:**Effective campaigns evoke genuine emotions and seek to connect with the audience on a deeper level.

4. **Adaptation and Flexibility:**The ability to adapt to market changes and be flexible in strategy is essential.

5. **Learning from Mistakes:**Failures can provide valuable lessons for future growth and success.

Conclusion: Integrating Learning into Future Strategies

Neuromarketing offers a window to understand and learn from successful campaigns and common mistakes. Integrating these lessons into future strategies allows brands to move forward with a deeper understanding of their consumers' needs and emotions, leading to more effective and authentic campaigns.

Chapter 22: Future Perspectives of Neuromarketing: Technological Advances and Emerging Trends

Neuromarketing is constantly evolving, driven by technological advances and emerging trends that are reshaping the way brands understand and connect with their consumers. In this chapter, we will explore future projections and innovations that could transform the field of neuromarketing.

Integration of Advanced Technologies in Neuromarketing Research

1. **Virtual Reality (VR) and Augmented Reality (AR):** VR and AR allow researchers to recreate realistic shopping environments to study consumer responses in simulated contexts.

2. **Biosensors and Portable Devices:** The incorporation of wearable devices and biosensors allows the collection of biometric data in real time, offering precise information about the consumer's physiological responses.

3. **Artificial Intelligence (AI) and Machine Learning:** AI makes it easier to analyze large volumes of data and develop more sophisticated algorithms to predict and understand consumer behavior.

Multisensory Approach and Consumer Experience

1. **Expanded Sensory Marketing:** Further exploration of multisensory influence is expected in neuromarketing, strategically integrating the senses to create more immersive and memorable experiences.

2. **Personalization at the Cognitive Level:** Using advanced technologies, brands will be able to personalize not only messages, but also the consumer's cognitive experience, adapting stimuli according to their psychological profile.

Ethics and Privacy in Future Neuromarketing

1. **Transparency and Consent:** Greater emphasis is expected on transparency and consent in neural data collection, ensuring privacy and ethics in the use of consumer information.

2. **Regulations and Guidelines:**As neuromarketing advances, stricter regulations are likely to emerge to safeguard the rights and privacy of individuals in relation to the brain information collected.

Neuromarketing and Digitalization of Commerce

1. **Strategies in Electronic Commerce:**The application of neuromarketing will intensify in digital environments, using data analysis to understand and optimize the user experience on online platforms.

2. **Brain-Computer Interaction (BCI):**The development of brain-computer interfaces will enable more direct interactions between the consumer's mind and technology, offering innovative opportunities for neuromarketing.

Adoption of Neuromarketing in Various Sectors and Contexts

1. **Health & Wellness:**Greater use of neuromarketing is expected to promote healthy habits and create wellness strategies, using neuroscientific techniques to motivate behavioral changes.

2. **Education and Learning:**The application of neuromarketing in education will focus on personalized strategies for teaching, adapting learning methods according to the brain activity of the students.

Conclusions: The Promising Future of Neuromarketing

The future of neuromarketing is full of technological advances and emerging trends that will transform the way brands understand and connect with their consumers.

Chapter 23: Neuromarketing and Personalization: The Tailored Consumer Experience

Neuromarketing has revolutionized the way brands interact with their consumers. In this chapter, we will explore how personalization, based on neuromarketing techniques, is shaping the consumer experience to adapt to their individual preferences.

Understanding Personalization in the Context of Neuromarketing

1. **Defining Personalization:**Personalization focuses on tailoring messages, products or services to meet the specific needs and preferences of each individual.

2. **Neuromarketing Approach:**Personalization in neuromarketing is based on a deep understanding of brain responses, allowing strategies to be adjusted to influence consumer behavior more effectively.

Neuromarketing Techniques for Personalization

1. **Biometric Data Analysis:**Collecting and analyzing biometric data, such as emotional response and brain activity, provides key insights to personalize interactions with consumers.

2. **Consumer Segmentation based on Cognitive Profiles:**The identification of cognitive and emotional patterns allows the creation of more precise consumer segments to personalize marketing strategies.

Tailored Consumer Experience: Impact and Benefits

1. **Deeper Emotional Connection:**Personalization creates a deeper emotional connection, as consumers feel understood and cared for based on their individual needs.

2. **Customer Loyalty and Loyalty:**Personalized experiences foster customer loyalty as they feel valued and are more likely to make repeat purchases and recommend the brand.

Personalization on Various Channels and Platforms

1. **Personalized Digital Marketing:**Personalization is applied in digital strategies, such as personalized content on websites, emails or targeted advertisements, adapted to consumer preferences.

2. **Personalization in the Physical Environment:**In physical environments, such as retail stores, strategies are implemented to personalize the shopping experience, from product layout to interaction with staff.

Challenges and Ethical Considerations

1. **Privacy and Consent:**Ensuring privacy and obtaining explicit consent to collect personal data is essential in personalization to avoid invasions of privacy.

2. **Transparency and Responsibility:**Brands must be transparent about how they use data and be responsible in the ethical use of consumer information to prevent potential abuse.

Future of Personalization in Neuromarketing

1. **Integration of Emerging Technologies:**Personalization is expected to benefit from the integration of AI, augmented reality, and other emerging technologies to improve accuracy and effectiveness.

2. **Continued Focus on Consumer Experience:**Personalization will continue to be a key focus in neuromarketing as brands seek to deliver more relevant and meaningful experiences to their consumers.

Conclusions: Transformative Impact of Personalization Neuromarketing

Personalization, driven by neuromarketing, has transformed the way brands interact with consumers, offering unique experiences tailored to individual preferences. By addressing ethical challenges and embracing emerging technologies, personalization will continue to be a critical pillar for customer loyalty and business success.

Chapter 24: Psychology of E-commerce: Keys to Maximize Online Sales

Electronic commerce, or e-commerce, is based on digital interaction with consumers. From the perspective of consumer psychology, maximizing sales in this environment is based on several pillars:

1. User Experience (UX): Ease of navigation, clarity in product presentation, and simplicity in the purchasing process are essential to generating a positive experience.

2. Design and Colors: Using colors and designs that resonate with your target audience can significantly influence purchasing decisions. Specific colors evoke emotions and can direct attention to key products.

3. Price Psychology: Strategies such as round numbers, discounted prices and price comparison can impact consumer perception of value.

4. Urgency and Scarcity: Creating a sense of urgency through time or stock limitations can stimulate quick purchasing decisions.

5. Personalization and Recommendations: Using algorithms that offer personalized recommendations based on browsing history and previous purchases can increase the relevance of the products presented.

6. Social Proof and Testimonials: Showing real customer testimonials and positive ratings can build trust and legitimacy in the buyer's mind.

7. Emotional Marketing Strategies: Appealing to consumer emotions through compelling stories or evocative images can have a profound impact on brand perception and purchasing decision.

8. Payment Page Optimization: Making the checkout process easier with clear steps and varied payment options can reduce cart abandonment rates.

9. Security and Transparency: Transmitting security in the protection of data and transactions is crucial to gaining consumer trust.

Conclusions: The Importance of Psychology in E-commerce

The effective application of consumer psychology in e-commerce can have a significant impact on sales. Understanding the motivations, behaviors and perceptions of online consumers can guide strategies that maximize user experience and ultimately drive conversions and customer loyalty.

Chapter 25: Sensorimotor Marketing: The Influence of Movement on Communication Strategies

Sensorimotor Marketing focuses on understanding how movement influences communication strategies to capture attention and generate emotional responses in consumers. Some key areas are explored here:

1. The Brain-Body Connection in Consumer Perception

Movement, whether in visual communication or physical experience, can activate specific areas of the brain, generating emotional and cognitive responses in consumers.

2. Movement-Based Communication Strategies

- **Dynamic Advertising:**Advertisements that incorporate elements of movement to attract attention and convey messages effectively.

- **Interactive Experiences:**Campaigns that invite consumers to actively participate, moving or interacting with the brand.

3. Neuromarketing and Sensorimotor Responses

- **Visual Stimulus and Movement:**Neuromarketing studies demonstrate how visual movement can capture attention and affect consumers' perception of a product or message.

- **Touch and Motion Experience:**Strategies that involve tactile experience, where movement can influence the perception of the quality or feel of a product.

4. Emotions and Movement in Communication

- **Emotional Expression Through Movement:**How movement can be used to convey emotions and generate deeper connections with consumers.

5. Sensorimotor Technology and Marketing

- **Augmented Reality and Virtual Reality:**The use of immersive technologies that involve physical movement to create more compelling and memorable experiences.

6. Impact of the Movement on Consumer Decision Making

- **Influence on Purchasing Behavior:**How movement can influence purchasing decisions, whether in the physical store or in digital environments.

7. Creation of Memorable Sensorimotor Experiences

- **Engagement Strategies:**Development of campaigns that involve movement to create sensorimotor experiences that remain in the consumer's memory.

Conclusions: Importance of Movement in Sensorimotor Marketing

Sensorimotor Marketing represents an evolution in communication strategies, recognizing the power of movement to capture attention, generate emotions and improve the consumer experience. Understanding and effectively applying how movement affects sensorimotor responses can be key to success in the modern marketing world.

Chapter 26: Neuroethics in Advertising: Reflections on the Ethical Impact of Campaigns

Neuroethics in advertising focuses on the evaluation of advertising practices from an ethical perspective, considering how advertising strategies can influence consumer behavior from a neuroscientific perspective. Here are some important reflections:

1. Ethics in Neuromarketing Research

- **Privacy and Consent:** The collection of brain and biometric data raises ethical concerns about privacy and the need to obtain informed consent.

- **Transparency in the Methodology:** It is crucial to disclose how neuromarketing data is collected and used to ensure transparency and public trust.

2. Ethics in the Use of Neuromarketing Techniques in Advertising

- **Manipulation and Freedom of Choice:** Advertising strategies based on knowledge of the brain raise questions about manipulation and the consumer's ability to make free decisions.

- **Brand Responsibility:** Brands have an ethical responsibility to use neuroscience in advertising in an ethical and respectful manner.

3. Ethics in the Creation of Advertising Content

- **Authenticity and Veracity:** Advertising campaigns must be authentic and truthful in the representation of products or services, avoiding exaggeration or misleading manipulation.

- **Impact on Mental Health:** Intensive advertising can have repercussions on consumers' mental health, raising ethical concerns about the influence on self-esteem and body perception.

4. Ethics in Segmentation and Directing the Public

- **Privacy and Segmentation:** Using data to segment and target specific audiences raises ethical questions about privacy and manipulation of preferences.

5. Ethics in the Evaluation of the Impact of Campaigns

- **Responsible Evaluation:**It is essential to evaluate the real impact of advertising campaigns, considering not only the commercial benefits but also the social and psychological impact.

Conclusions: The Commitment to Neuroethics in Advertising

Neuroethics in advertising is an evolving field, where ethical responsibility and the balance between commercial objectives and consumer well-being are crucial. Continuous reflection and commitment to ethical and transparent advertising practices are essential to building relationships of trust with consumers and society at large.

Chapter 27: Neuromarketing and Customer Loyalty: Strategies to Maintain Long-Term Relationships

Customer loyalty is essential for any business, and neuromarketing can offer effective strategies to maintain lasting relationships with consumers. Below are some key strategies:

1. Customer Knowledge Through Neuromarketing

- **Preference Analysis:**Use neuromarketing techniques to understand customer preferences and adapt offers according to their needs and desires.

- **Precise Segmentation:**Segment customers according to their neuropsychological profiles to personalize loyalty strategies.

2. Customer Experience and Neuropsychology

- **Creating Memorable Experiences:**Use neuropsychological principles to design experiences that generate positive emotions and lasting memories in clients.

- **Customer Support:**Strategies based on personalized attention, which trigger positive emotional responses, such as gratitude and trust.

3. Neuroscience in Customer Communication

- **Persuasive Communication:**Use neuromarketing techniques in messages that activate emotional areas of the brain, generating emotional attachment to the brand.

- **Consistency in Communication:**Maintain a consistent and emotionally engaging message at all customer contact points.

4. Emotional Loyalty and Neuromarketing

- **Generation of Feeling of Belonging:**Strategies that encourage emotional loyalty, such as loyalty programs based on emotional rewards.

- **Brand Rating:**Use neuromarketing techniques to reinforce brand valuation and its association with positive experiences.

5. Use of Technology in Customer Loyalty

- **Technological Personalization:**Use technology to personalize offers, reminders and experiences tailored to individual neuropsychological preferences.

6. Neuromarketing Evaluation of Loyalty Success

- **Neuromarketing Indicators:**Evaluate the effectiveness of loyalty strategies using neuropsychological metrics, such as emotional response to campaigns.

Conclusions: Importance of Neuromarketing Loyalty

Building customer loyalty through neuromarketing involves understanding the consumer's underlying motivations and offering emotionally relevant and personalized experiences. Focusing on emotional connection and adapting to individual needs can lead to long-lasting customer relationships.

Chapter 28: Neuromarketing and Gamification: How to Turn the Shopping Experience into a Game

Gamification is the integration of game elements into non-game environments to encourage participation and engagement. In the field of neuromarketing, gamification strategies are used to improve the shopping experience and promote consumer interaction. Here are the key points:

1. Fundamentals of Gamification in Neuromarketing

- **Intrinsic motivation:**Gamification takes advantage of the individual's intrinsic motivation towards the game, activating emotional areas of the brain to generate engagement.

- **Influence on Behavior:**Gamification can influence purchasing decisions by creating interactive experiences that stimulate positive emotional responses.

2. Elements of Gamification in the Shopping Experience

- **Challenges and Objectives:**Establish challenges, goals or achievements within the purchasing process to maintain consumer interest.

- **Rewards and Recognitions:**Offer tangible or intangible rewards to motivate and reward participation.

3. Neuroscience and Effects on User Experience

- **Emotional Response:**Gamification can generate positive emotions, such as pleasure and satisfaction, that are associated with the shopping experience.

- **Dopamine Increase:**Playful elements can activate the release of dopamine, generating feelings of achievement and motivation.

4. Gamification Strategies in Neuromarketing

- **Application in Online and Offline Environments:**Both in physical stores and on online platforms, gamification can improve the customer experience.

- **Personalization of the Experience:**Adapt gamification strategies according to individual consumer preferences and behaviors.

5. Impact on Customer Loyalty and Retention

- **Increased Participation:**Gamification can increase consumer interaction, fostering brand loyalty.

- **Generation of Memorable Experiences:**Gamified shopping experiences can remain engraved in the consumer's memory, generating a lasting impact.

Conclusions: Importance of Gamification in Neuromarketing

Gamification in neuromarketing is a powerful tool to improve the purchasing experience by involving emotions, motivations and playful experiences in the consumption process. Strategic and careful design of gamification can enhance consumer interaction and create stronger bonds with brands.

Chapter 29: Experiential Marketing: Creating Memorable Experiences at the Brain Level

Experiential marketing focuses on creating impactful experiences that generate positive and memorable emotions in consumers. These experiences not only seek to sell a product or service, but also connect emotionally with customers. Below are the key aspects:

1. Focus on Emotion and Experience

- **Emotional Stimulus:**Experiential marketing seeks to awaken emotions through sensory, cognitive and affective experiences.

- **Emotional Connection:**It seeks to connect with consumers on a deeper level, creating memories and positive associations with the brand.

2. Creation of Meaningful Experiences

- **Sensory Elements:**The use of visual, auditory, tactile and olfactory stimuli to create a multisensory experience that impacts the brain.

- **Narrative and Storytelling:**Tell stories that connect emotionally with consumers and make them feel part of a unique experience.

3. Impact on the Brain and Consumer Response

- **Brain Activation:**Experiential marketing seeks to activate areas of the brain associated with emotions, memory and decision making.

- **Generation of Lasting Memories:**Exceptional experiences are more likely to be remembered, generating a positive association with the brand.

4. Experiential Marketing Strategies

- **Events and Activations:**Organize events or activations that actively involve consumers in the experience.

- **Personalization:**Tailor experiences to individual tastes and preferences to generate a more significant impact.

5. Emotional Connection and Consumer Loyalty

- **Long Term Loyalty:**Memorable experiences create an emotional bond that can lead to sustained brand loyalty.

- **Differentiation in the Market:**Brands that offer unique and meaningful experiences stand out in a saturated market.

Conclusions: Importance of Experiential Marketing

Experiential marketing goes beyond the commercial transaction, it seeks to create emotional connections that last in the consumer's memory. The generation of memorable experiences at the brain level contributes to strengthening the relationship between the brand and the consumer, influencing perception, preference and loyalty towards it.

Chapter 30: Integration of Neuromarketing in Business Strategies: Keys to Business Success

Neuromarketing offers valuable insights for business strategies by better understanding consumer motivations, perceptions and behaviors. Its integration into corporate strategies can be key to commercial success. Below are the essential points:

1. Deep Level Consumer Understanding

- **Behavior Analysis:**Use neuromarketing techniques to understand how consumers react to marketing stimuli and the factors that influence their decision making.

- **Construction of Consumer Profiles:**Integrate neuromarketing data to create more precise and detailed consumer profiles, allowing for more specific and effective strategies.

2. Personalization and Customer Experience

- **Custom Strategies:**Use neuromarketing information to personalize experiences and messages, increasing relevance and impact on each customer.

- **Design of Memorable Experiences:**Implement strategies based on neuromarketing to create experiences that generate positive and memorable emotions.

3. Optimization of Products and Services

- **Perception-Based Design:**Use neuromarketing information to develop products and services that align with consumer perceptions and preferences.

- **Product Testing:**Use neuromarketing techniques in product testing to better understand consumer preferences and reactions to different attributes.

4. Communication and Marketing Strategies

- **Effective Messages:**Use neuromarketing principles to create messages that have an emotional impact and generate a deeper connection with the target audience.

- **Marketing Channel Optimization:**Integrate neuromarketing knowledge to select the most effective marketing channels to reach the target audience.

5. Innovation and Continuous Adaptation

- **Adaptation to Changes:**Use neuromarketing information to quickly adapt to changing market trends and consumer preferences.

- **Data-Driven Innovation:**Use neuromarketing data and analysis to drive innovation and the development of more effective business strategies.

Conclusions: Importance of the Integration of Neuromarketing in Business Strategies

Integrating neuromarketing into business strategies allows for a more consumer-centric approach, providing valuable insights to better understand and meet market needs. This strategic integration can be decisive for commercial success by generating more attractive products, more effective messages and more memorable experiences for consumers.